PHYSICALLY IN

MENTALLY OUT

NAVIGATING YOUR EXIT FROM WATCHTOWER

Bethany Leger

Author's note
My personal experiences included in this book were written in good faith, presented with a desire to be fair and honest, and for educational purposes.

Disclaimer
This book is not intended for providing psychological or medical services. If expert assistance or counseling is needed, the services of a competent professional should be sought.

For Jon, my rock

TABLE OF CONTENTS

4 – THE THERAPY PART   54

5 – THE PART WHERE YOU'RE FREE   65

INTRODUCTION

Meet the PIMO

I was one of Jehovah's Witnesses for 30 years. After I left, I became an activist on YouTube for a year. During that time, I received hundreds of emails from viewers. Over half of those emails came from frustrated Jehovah's Witnesses who wanted to leave the organization but were keeping up appearances for their family. These closeted non-believers are known in the Ex-Jehovah's Witnesses community as "PIMO" – Physically In, Mentally Out.

These PIMOs want to be free—they want to relax after work and sleep in on weekends. They want to have sex and roll around in the dirt pit of debauchery. I'm sure I'll be slammed for that, because it's one of the many accusations PIMOs resent most. *No, I don't want to leave so I can be bad,* they say. The fact that they feel pressured to defend their moral compass at all, however, highlights the greater issue.

It doesn't matter if a PIMO is sexually repressed and wants to be "bad", or if their longing for freedom has nothing to do with sex.

They don't believe in the doctrine anymore (or never did). They don't trust Watchtower's leadership. Others just want to be able to grow their own facial hair without being punished. PIMOs ultimately want the same thing: the freedom to think for themselves. So, why do they stay? They know that if they leave the organization, then their devout Jehovah's Witness family will shun them.[1]

If you're reading this as a PIMO, the good news is your situation is not hopeless. I, along with countless former PIMOs, have successfully transitioned out of Watchtower, and I can help you navigate your own exit. The bad news? If you're not a fan of tough love, you bought the wrong book.

Spoiler Alert

I can tell you now, PIMO, that *you are never going to receive permission to be yourself.* Your family is never going to give you their blessing, and if your happiness depends on their approval, you're going to be miserable for a long time. Think about it—they're devoted to an organization that doesn't allow *them* to be themselves. How can you, then, expect them to nurture your authenticity?

I realize that it's sensitive territory when you start talking about someone else's family, and I'm by no means minimizing your struggle. Watchtower is squeezing you between a rock and a hard place. Assuming one loves their family and shares a relatively healthy relationship with them, no one wants to take actions they know are going to result in permanent estrangement. I didn't set out to break my mother's heart when I disassociated, but I also never asked to be raised in a group that would expect my mother to choose them over her own child. That is the crucial point I hope, if nothing else, you glean from this book: that just because you were born into dysfunction, doesn't make it your responsibility to repeat or endure it.

The Baptism Card

This is usually where detractors will pull the baptism card: *Why are you complaining? It was your decision to get baptized.*

Let's clear something up.

In the United States, at least, minors are not permitted to consume alcohol, vote, get married, or drive a motor vehicle without careful legal stipulations. Yet, Watchtower has no problem manipulating minors into committing to something of which they are developmentally incapable of grasping the full implications. As a minor, I did not possess the developmental capacity to process the ideology that was imposed on me, or how it would gerrymander the family bonds I assumed were nonnegotiable. Still, throughout my formative years in the Watchtower petri dish, I was taught that baptism was not only a good idea, but one that was *necessary* for me to survive the end of the world.[2]

Shunning is a bomb that a child can't possibly comprehend until it's dropped long after their ill-advised baptism, when the impact tremor rips through their adult life. By exploiting a child's need for love and security, coupled with the threat of being murdered at Armageddon if you're not a Jehovah's Witness, Watchtower convinced us to get baptized through undue influence. End of story.

If you want to accuse me of playing the Blame Game, you would only be half-right. I place the responsibility for my baptism squarely on the shoulders of the adults in my life at the time, because as a minor, I never should have been handed the keys to the car. That "decision" should never have been mine to make when they knew it carried ramifications that could affect me for the rest of my life. However, as an adult, I now understand what happened, and I can take the reins of my life moving forward.

The First Step

I believe the first step toward your freedom is education: specifically, educating yourself about narcissistic abuse. You can logically dismantle Watchtower doctrine and pat yourself on the back, but you will still have the emotional component to grapple with—your love for your family and any friendships you've forged over the years. It's tempting to believe that unlocking the Rubik's Cube of Watchtower indoctrination is enough to wake them up and secure your relationships, but the roots of manipulation run deeper than whatever kooky ideas Charles Taze Russell left in his wake.

Watchtower is an extremely narcissistic organization. Jehovah's Witnesses are taught that they are superior to believers of all other religions, and if you ever leave the organization, no one will love you and you will die. When you understand that Watchtower's modus operandi is identical to that of an abusive relationship, you can recognize the signs and protect yourself. In time, you will stop internalizing these messages of fear, guilt, and shame, and you will step into your power, consequences be damned.

The Power of the PIMO

"Step into your power" is a buzz phrase you've probably heard before. It means different things to different people, but in this context, I'm talking about setting boundaries and reclaiming your life; you are unabashedly yourself and fear of reprisal no longer dictates your decisions. It also means that you, and every PIMO out there, holds the power to instigate massive change. For every PIMO who finally walks out, another PIMO is inspired to do the same, and it creates a chain reaction.

Wow—I had no idea Brother Covert felt the same way I did.

Sister Incognito snapped? I feel you, girl!

Of course, it is precisely this level of Stalinist pretense in the organization that makes it difficult to decipher who is PIMO in the first place. Any PIMO knows all too well the risk involved in confronting someone they suspect is PIMO about their secret feelings or doubts. But the fact is, you don't know how your balls-out, shameless exit is going to affect someone who is on the verge of doing the same. You'll have street cred for life.

Shunning

Over the last century, Watchtower has fought for its religious freedoms in both local and Supreme Courts. It is, therefore, the height of hypocrisy for Watchtower to argue for its religious freedom only to punish and ostracize members who no longer believe in their doctrine. The July 2009 *Awake!* article, "Is it Wrong to Change Your Religion?", states: "No one should be forced to worship in a way that he finds unacceptable or be made to choose between his beliefs and his family."[3] This ironic statement, featured in their own literature, blatantly contradicts their shunning policy.

I got involved with online activism because I was fed up with the silence and shame that characterizes the lives of those who leave. When you grow up in the organization, the disturbing trend of erasing people is normalized from a young age. Members of my own family—siblings and extended relatives—were shunned for years; as a child who had unconditional love for her family, I didn't understand why it was considered acceptable for the congregation to treat someone I loved as if they were dead. I, in turn, learned to shun others because those were the rules.

Everyone wants to believe their family will be the exception to the rule, that their loved ones won't shun them—and to be clear, I don't believe they would of their own volition. Watchtower is solely responsible for instituting and pressuring families to enforce the shunning policy. Unfortunately, when your devout family cuts ties with you out of misguided loyalty to the organization, they become active participants in perpetuating this cycle of abuse.

When you muster up the courage to admit to yourself that you are no different—meaning you are in the same potential shunning boat as everyone else—you will stop viewing your situation entirely through the cultural lens of the organization. We all do it—when faced with the threat of shunning, we try to comfort ourselves by comparing the leniency of our family to others in the congregation, or speculate that we might get a break based on our track record of being a good son or daughter.

This wishful thinking is a natural response to the inhumane prospect of shunning, not unlike the Denial Stage in Elizabeth Kübler-Ross' Five Stages of Grief (i.e. Denial, Anger, Bargaining, Depression, and Acceptance). Rather, you will begin to see your situation for what it is: You're in an abusive relationship, and the standard control tactics will be used when you attempt to break free. Like any skilled abuser, Watchtower puts the onus on the shunned individual to make things right. It is when you understand how abusive dynamics work that you will stop laboring under the misconception that the relationship is yours to fix.

The Purpose of this Book

I'm not an unreasonable person. I realize that a swift exit is not always possible for a PIMO due to health problems, arranging care for aging parents, or some other mitigating circumstance. Maybe you're a minor. Maybe you want to be on stronger financial footing before you make your break, or maybe you simply can't handle the emotional upheaval at this stage of your life. I understand there are grey areas in life and I wouldn't expect anyone to blindly follow my advice when I don't have to live with the results. All I'm proposing is for PIMOs to conduct an honest inventory of their life and determine how their current actions and choices are aligning with their dreams of freedom.

Actions, boundaries, choices, dreams. In the following chapters, I will explore these concepts in greater detail and how I believe they apply to the PIMO. Since it's impossible for me to know every PIMO's circumstances, however, this book is not so much a universal manual for how to leave Watchtower as it is about how to take care of yourself through the inevitable fallout. Nor can you expect me to teach you some secret handshake so you can stay in stealth mode with other PIMOs. Yes, I believe in your inherent worth. I believe that you deserve to heal, and I believe your life has purpose, something that excites you and fills your lungs with the fresh air of freedom and possibility. But, you sure as hell are not going to find it while hiding at the Kingdom Hall.

Instead, this book will help you to:

- Gain the confidence you need to give the proverbial—or real—finger to others' expectations

- Reframe your experience and see a potentially negative consequence from a different angle
- Reconnect with (yes!) your "old" personality—the one that made you cool and interesting AF before you had to change for Watchtower

Most importantly, you will learn how to put Watchtower in your rearview mirror and create the life you long for. Here's to stepping out of the shadows and burning bright.

THE FUN PART

Visualization

You've left Watchtower. What happens next?

You don't have Saturday morning service anymore. Do you go out for breakfast and make love to a stack of pancakes? Or do you stay home with your boo and make love *in* the stack of pancakes? (I don't judge.)

> What's your next adventure?
> Where are you?
> What are you doing?
> What are the sights, sounds, smells, tastes?
> What happens next month? Next year? Five years from now?
> What is your dream?

For some of you, this is new and exciting, and for some of you, I can see the eye-roll. As a life coach, I'm aware of the image that people have of the schmaltzy motivational speaker. So long as these individuals aren't exploiting audiences out of their life savings, or isolating them from their family, I say, to each their own. But if you're going to maintain the attitude that dreaming is for suckers, you might as well stay in Watchtower, where dreams go to die.

Every PIMO dreams of being somewhere else, doing something else. Your dream is simply your desire for change, and change requires action. When you break down what it will take to achieve your dreams into small, actionable steps, the exercise of indulging your dreams looks less like self-help drivel and more like basic math.

I also understand that it might be challenging to articulate your dreams when you were taught it was dangerous or selfish to have them. That's because your dreams, your wants and needs, don't serve Watchtower. The only person who can convince you that your dream is silly, impossible, or that you don't deserve it, is you. No one—not Watchtower, your family, or me—has the right to question your potential.

Now, back to your dream. I want you to take a few minutes to think about it and describe it in detail. Ask yourself the following questions:

What do I want?
Who do I want to be?
What would I do if I knew I couldn't fail?
What does my ideal day/week/life look like?

Watchtower placed all sorts of limits on what I can do. What if those limits were removed?

You can also try what I call The Meeting Trick: when your mind inevitably wanders during the weekly meeting, what do you think about? I don't care if you're dreaming of eating Chipotle and getting laid. Keep the dream alive.

After you've put your dream in writing, hold onto it. No, not just the dream—the actual paper. Put it on your desk, your nightstand, or your fridge. Keep a copy on your computer (if you don't share your computer with another Jehovah's Witness) or text it to yourself. Let it be your guide/anchor/motivation as you devise your exit strategy.

SMART Goals

Once you have a clear dream or vision for your life after Watchtower, you can create goals to achieve it. Maybe you learned about SMART goals in school, or in a professional development course at work. It stands for goals that are Specific, Measurable, Achievable, Realistic, and Time-Sensitive.

Let's say your dream is to become a doctor. Which of the following goals is more powerful?

#1 – I want to go to college.

#2 – I will earn my PhD and complete a residency program by June 1st, 2030.

The first goal is vague, but the second goal is SMART. Once you create your SMART goal, you can then create a list of action steps to achieve your goal:

- Research colleges and universities
- Call the admissions office
- Schedule an appointment with an academic advisor
- Apply for financial aid
- Go to class
- Study for exams

You can create even smaller, short-term goals within a long-term goal: *I will earn my undergraduate degree by June 1, 2024.*

Some goals may be more abstract, such as wanting to gain more confidence in social situations. How would you make this goal SMART? How would you measure your progress? Below are possible options for SMART goals:

I will ask at least one of my coworkers to join me for lunch this Friday.

I will attend yoga every Tuesday and Thursday this month.

I will participate in Trivia Night at my local brewery next Wednesday.

Your dreams and goals should be meaningful to *you*. If your dreams and goals don't resonate with you, if they feel like something you "should" do rather than something you truly want to do, you are a lot less likely to follow through.

In the space below, I want you to create at least three SMART goals that are going to help you achieve your dream.

1.

____

2.

____

3.

____

The "Old" Personality

As a Jehovah's Witness, you're told to "strip off the old personality", or your past ways. Considering a born-in Jehovah's Witness isn't given the chance to develop their distinct personality, this command has less to do with renouncing an ungodly lifestyle and more to do with rejecting everything that makes you an individual.[1] Former Jehovah's Witnesses and PIMOs alike describe Watchtower as having stolen their youth, killed their dreams, etc. Watchtower even prides itself on being able to manipulate converts into abandoning their careers and talents to serve Watchtower's interests.[2] Instead, I want you to reconnect with the parts of your "old" personality that didn't fit into the Watchtower mold—the personality characteristics, beliefs, or hobbies you had to neglect or suppress.

I'm not suggesting you regress to a time or part of you that you no longer identify with. Likewise, when I talk about dreams and goals, my purpose isn't to be contrarian—I don't want you to be something or someone you're not for the sake of kicking against Watchtower. I believe our experiences help shape who we are, and I wouldn't discount how your unique experience in the organization informed who you are today. Perhaps your sincere conviction at one time moved you to give up drugs, or maybe you developed an appreciation for teamwork from helping others in the congregation. These changes may very well have had a positive impact throughout your life.

It's also possible that you've become hardened trying to live up to Watchtower's unreasonable standards, but it wouldn't be fair to say that you have no standards of your own. In this way, I want you to give yourself the credit that Watchtower assumes for itself and retire the belief that you're broken or lost without them. Remember, you're not a good person because you're a Jehovah's Witness—you're just a good person.

I wouldn't even consider this kind of inner work to be "self-improvement" as much as self-exploration. You are not lacking. Rather, the purpose of this exercise is to integrate *all* the components that make you who you are, and in some cases, that means going back before you can move forward.

To put on the "old" personality, consider the following questions. You may find that your "old" personality is right at the surface, readily accessible; you may need to give each question some thought. Either way, *please,* have fun with it! You are not being tasked with a Watchtower article that you need to laboriously dissect with your highlighter. There are no right or wrong answers, so don't censor yourself.

What do you enjoy doing?

____

____

____

____

____

____

____

____

What were your favorite subjects in school?

When you were a child, what did you want to be when you grew up?

____

____

____

____

____

____

____

____

____

When was a time you were truly happy?

What are your special skills/talents?

____

____

____

____

____

____

____

____

____

What are you good at that you never got paid for?

Is there something you always wanted to do, but due to circumstances, you put it aside?

____

____

____

____

____

____

____

____

____

Is there a talent, gift, or ability you have that you never developed, but could or would like to?

____

____

____

____

____

____

____

____

____

What is unique about you?

____

____

____

____

____

____

____

____

____

What is one thing about you that no one else knows?

What are your unresolved dreams?

____

____

____

____

____

____

____

____

____

Who are the people (living or dead) you most admire and why?

What comes naturally to you?

____

____

____

____

____

____

____

____

____

What accomplishments are you proud of?

Is there something you feel called to do, even if it doesn't seem realistic?

____

____

____

____

____

____

____

____

____

What parts of yourself do you feel need expression (i.e. artistic, athletic, entrepreneurial, sexual)?

What legacy do you want to leave behind?

____

____

____

____

____

____

____

____

____

Home Alone

Remember when your parents went away for the weekend and allowed you to stay at home alone for the first time? The minute they backed out of the driveway, you went straight for the ice cream, the phone, the porn, you skipped the Sunday meeting (sweet, sweet freedom!), jumped off the roof with your idiot friends, lost your virginity, binge-watched *America's Next Top Model*, got high, slept all weekend, or did absolutely, gloriously, nothing.

I experienced a similar feeling when I left the organization. The noise of Watchtower was suddenly gone: no more meetings, service, constant rushing and busy work, no more fakery between me and the other congregation inmates. I distinctly recall sitting in the silence of my living room, thinking, *Holy shit, I'm free.* As a PIMO, you long for your independence from Watchtower. It's common, however, for someone to leave Watchtower and express that they are overwhelmed by their newfound freedom. They're afraid of failure, or a sobering life experience has put them in a different headspace.

I'm not trying to romanticize youth, or give you permission to renege on your adult responsibilities. I only want you to revive your innate sense of experimentation and exploration that Watchtower stifled over the years. That first taste of freedom from your parents was exhilarating, and yes, you probably did some dumb stuff—but you survived. When left to your own devices, you managed not to set the house on fire (let's hope), you remembered to feed the dog and lock the doors, and you kept yourself alive.

When Watchtower is finally out of the picture, how are you going to seize your freedom? Pick your motto: carpe diem, grab the bull by the horns, get in the game. Your life starts now.

THE NOT-SO-FUN PART

The House

I remember the night I debated whether to officially disassociate from the organization. I was curled up in the fetal position sobbing uncontrollably. However, I wasn't crying because I was sad at the prospect of leaving Watchtower. Standing on the precipice of freedom, visualizing that I had shed the title of "Jehovah's Witness" and the life that comes with it, was thrilling. Rather, I knew that disassociation was the kiss of death, and I might never see my parents again.

I struggled to wrap my brain around either of these outcomes. I tried frantically to piece all the implications of the puzzle together knowing that I couldn't possibly see the whole picture at that point. When you're a Jehovah's Witness, you have certainty, an answer for everything. Even though waiting around for the ending was boring, at least you knew what the ending was. Suddenly, it was the other way around.

I had already been inactive for six months, but merely fading from the organization felt like I was doing patchwork on a house that I didn't want to live in—I was tired of putting my conversations with my parents through a Watchtower-approved filter, or keeping up pretenses on the rare occasion that someone from the congregation dropped by. I wanted to build a new house, a new life for myself, but was immobilized by fear and resentment. Then, in the throes of my ugly cry, it hit me: if I don't disassociate, fear and resentment will always rule my life.

Before I could rebuild, I had to burn the house down.

Know Your "Stuff"

As a born-in PIMO, your house was built by other people—your family and the congregation. They constructed a framework of rules and expectations, then filled each room with their own brand of crazy: maybe there was alcoholism, physical or sexual abuse, fanaticism or perfectionism. Maybe your home life was near idyllic, but being a Jehovah's Witness, your parents' love for you came with the condition that you remain a Jehovah's Witness. Whatever the case, your liberation from Watchtower is going to require you to confront these family dynamics so you can distinguish the parts of your identity you inherited from these outside architects, from those that are, in fact, your own.

This is vital due to the threat of projection: When you attempt to leave the organization, you are going to become the dumping ground for your family's "stuff." They are going to project their own guilt, shame, anger, and confusion onto you so you can be the Bad Guy and they don't have to face the uncomfortable reality that "the truth" is not the truth. In their defense, they've also been abused by Watchtower and are possibly resisting their own waking up process. You're challenging their worldview and deeply cherished beliefs; you have to imagine that this confrontation is akin to hitting them upside the head with a two by four. Again, as sad and frustrating as it is, you're going to need to become skilled at discerning what "stuff" is truly yours and what belongs to your family so that you don't end up owning their problems.

Consider the Source

As I mentioned at the outset of this book, the first step toward your freedom is educating yourself about narcissistic abuse. Disclaimer: I'm not a doctor. I wouldn't even call myself an expert. I've only researched the subject extensively and applied what I've learned to my own experience. I'm not making any sweeping claims that your parent/child/cousin has a clinical diagnosis of Narcissistic Personality Disorder or suggesting that you slap unwarranted labels on your loved ones.

When I talk about narcissistic abuse, I'm referring to Watchtower's legacy of emotional and psychological manipulation. My issue is not, nor has it ever been, with Jehovah's Witnesses as individuals. I maintain that they are equal victims of Watchtower's central authority, the Governing Body, and any chemical or genetic predisposition they may have for a legitimate mental disorder is a different argument. However, because your family is under Watchtower's influence, your exit will inevitably provoke a narcissistic response.

What is narcissistic abuse? According to *Psychology Today*, common tactics include:[1]

- Lying
- Denial
- Avoidance
- Gaslighting
- Blame, Guilt, Shame
- Intimidation
- Playing the victim

My intention is not so much to reiterate the exhaustive amount of material on the subject as it is to stress its importance in the context of the PIMO transition. The initial phase of your exit is the most challenging, and understanding what's happening in real time will help you to stay grounded during the shit storm.

The Script

Former Jehovah's Witnesses will refer to the prescribed conversations they had while they were still in the organization as "the script"; we had our own language and expectations for conversations with outsiders and with each other. When you deviate from the script and express your own opinion, it makes things awkward because you're not parroting Watchtower rhetoric. However, there's a separate script for your family, a role you're expected to play within your unique family dynamics.

There's a good chance that you're the Responsible One, PIMO; you've always brought honor to the family and never rocked the boat. I was the Responsible One, so much so that if I could go back in time, I would punch myself in the face. I had a predictable pattern of behavior; never in a million years did my parents expect me to do something so rebellious, so shocking, as disassociate. Likewise, when you stop following the script your family wrote for you, they won't know how to respond. It's at this critical juncture between asserting your independence from Watchtower and asserting your independence from your family's expectations that you forever alter the dynamic.

Rewriting the Script—Boundaries

When your family sees that you're wriggling free of Watchtower's grip, they'll resort to the family script in a last-ditch effort to regain control. They might use guilt trips, feign concern for your mental health, or demand you come to your senses—anything to get you to follow the script again. When you change your reaction to one that they don't expect, when you change your usual words and behaviors, you're rewriting the script at the cellular level.

How do you rewrite the script? Boundaries.

This is another subject you can find a wealth of information on with a simple Google search, and one that needn't share a direct correlation to narcissistic abuse. Having boundaries simply means you've created guidelines for acceptable behavior. Boundaries exist in school, the workplace, and in healthy relationships. In this context, establishing and enforcing boundaries is an essential part of rewriting your script.

There are going to be several opportunities in your exit to follow the old script: face-to-face conversations, text messages, phone conversations, or letters. It is vital for you to establish your boundaries in these situations and enforce them during any interactions moving forward. Your goal isn't to be combative – make it clear that you're coming from a place of mutual respect. However, if they violate your boundaries, or refuse to extend the same respect you're extending to them, protect yourself and end the conversation. (Note: If you do decide to end the conversation or if you determine that it's necessary to go "no contact," make sure that you're cutting your losses in the name of maintaining boundaries, and *not* because you're adopting the same narcissistic behaviors, i.e. "they have to think/act/be the same as me." This would make you no better than Watchtower.)

Below are some common "old script" tendencies along with "new script" responses that you can use as you establish your boundaries.

If your "old script" tendency is to:

- *Fight dirty?* **Bite your tongue.**
  You don't want to engage in ad hominem attacks, especially if you know the other person is prone to doing the same. Instead, your mellow mood will throw them—how is it that you're becoming *more* peaceful when you're falling into the hands of Satan?

- *Keep the peace?* **Be direct, but not antagonistic.**
  You clearly reject the unreasonable behavior, but are willing to engage in respectful discourse.

- *Bottle your emotions?* **"Let it out", but do so consciously.**
  You're expressing yourself for the benefit of releasing these emotions, but with the understanding that anything you say or do could be used against you.

- *Debate?* **Save your breath.**
  This is particularly challenging when you're desperate to wake the other person up, but you can't force someone to wake up who isn't ready to. By proposing that you both agree to disagree, it shows you're more interested in the relationship than changing their mind.

- *Rescue?* **Let it go.**
  It's not your responsibility to save your family from themselves. You can have compassion for their personal history or inner demons, but it's not your job to convince them that Watchtower is exploiting them if they're resisting this information. Again, you can't force someone to wake up.

Watchtower doesn't respect boundaries. The elders insert themselves into members' private lives, and this behavior is modeled for the rest of the congregation. You can physically remove yourself from your parents' home or stop going to meetings, but until you set clear boundaries, you risk getting sucked back into the drama. When you establish and enforce your standards for acceptable behavior, you teach others how to treat you.

Other thoughts:

- Twisting the facts is another classic narcissistic abuse tactic. If your family tries to pull the Watchtower line that *you* are shunning/disowning them, call it out. Your family doesn't want to shun you; it goes against their humanity and better judgment. Instead, by twisting the facts to make it look like you're the aggressor, Watchtower is letting your family off the hook from doing the right thing. You are rejecting Watchtower, *not* your family, and don't let them tell you otherwise.

- Keep a log or journal of your conversations with the other person so they can't gaslight you, i.e. make you question your own memory. Your purpose isn't to keep a tit-for-tat going, but to separate the truth from the lies.

- Resist the urge to insult. Name-calling detracts from your original message and reinforces the erroneous belief that people who leave are incapable of behaving in a dignified manner. Instead, beat them at their own game and heap those coals. Your civilized behavior may "win them over without a word" (see what I did there?).

Fade or Disassociate?

You may feel that I made things unnecessarily hard on myself by choosing to disassociate. I've spoken with many former Jehovah's Witnesses who chose to fade, or slowly stop participating in congregation activities, rather than formally revoke their membership. The fact is, there are pros and cons to both options.

Some feel that disassociation would make them an instigator; it's an aggressive move that will ensure estrangement from their family. Others feel that refusing to write a letter of disassociation is a refusal to play by Watchtower's rules. However, proponents feel that disassociation sends a clear message, and may motivate others to investigate the reasons for making such a bold move. I can appreciate both arguments, and the bottom line is, you should do whatever is going to leave you feeling empowered. For me, disassociation was empowering because it was my way of cutting ties with an ideology and identity that was imposed on me.

Dominique Moceanu, Olympic champion and member of the Magnificent Seven, describes the moment her parents decided she was going to be a gymnast; she was six months old. Her mother was doing laundry and lifted her up to the clothesline. When she gripped the line and managed to hang on, her life was planned for her.[2] As soon as I learned to say the words "Mama" and "Papa," I learned the word "Jehovah," and my entire life was wrapped up in a predetermined package.

Disassociating was my symbolic "Return to Sender" moment. Had I faded, I would still feel tethered to Watchtower, even if it was in name only. Critics might say my name is probably still floating around on the roster somewhere due to Watchtower's unscrupulous record-keeping, and they might be right. Regardless, the ritual of handing in my disassociation letter and hearing the chains unlock was victory enough for me.

Cost/Benefit Analysis

PIMOs devise their exit strategy based on different variables. Some PIMOs are resigned to the fact that they will be shunned, but build their foxhole before they leave: they save money, arrange to live with "worldly" family, or build a support network of some sort. Other PIMOs, sadly, wait until a devout aging parent passes away. There are PIMOs who are financially independent—perhaps with a supportive spouse and family of their own—who still hold out hope that their family of origin will wake up before they take any decisive action.

With any change, there's a benefit, payoff, cost, and loss. Applying the Cost/Benefit Analysis model to your situation can help you determine your priorities.

- *What is the **benefit** of making the change?*
- *What is the **payoff** for not making the change?*
- *What is it **costing** you to not make the change?*
- *What **loss** will you experience if you make the change?*

In this context, the change is leaving Watchtower. Bare minimum, your Cost/Benefit Analysis will look something like this:

- *What is the **benefit** of making the change?* → *Freedom from Watchtower*
- *What is the **payoff** for not making the change?* → *A relationship with my family*
- *What is it **costing** you to not make the change?* → *Freedom from Watchtower*
- *What **loss** will you experience if you make the change?* → *A relationship with my family*

Again, I don't know your personal circumstances. If the details were fleshed out, your Cost/Benefit Analysis may include any of the following:

- *What is the **benefit** of making the change?* → *Freedom from Watchtower's manipulation and mind control; freedom from meetings, service, and conventions; freedom to explore beloved hobbies; freedom to date a non-Jehovah's Witness and potentially find the love of my life*
- *What is the **payoff** for not making the change?* → *I'm not shunned; My family is happy/proud/at peace; I don't have to experience the stress that comes with leaving while also having to work and/or provide for a family*
- *What is it **costing** you to not make the change?* → *My mental and emotional health; my chances of finding a compatible partner; a fulfilling life where I get to do the things that bring me joy*
- *What **loss** will you experience if you make the change?* → *My family's approval; a place to live; my status/identity as an elder or pioneer; my current friends; my job (if working for another Jehovah's Witness)*

You can also ask yourself the following questions:

- *What exactly is it about this change that is challenging for me?*
- *What fears or concerns do I have around this change?*

- *What's holding me back from making this change?*
- *The worst happens (insert worst fear here). Then what?*
- *What could go wrong?*
- *What could go right?*

According to social-learning theorist Julian Rotter, if we believe more strongly that the outcomes of our actions are contingent on what we do, we have an *internal locus of control*. If we believe that the outcomes of our actions are contingent on environmental factors, we have an *external locus of control*.[3] In other words, we either believe that we have the power to make things happen and effect change, or we believe that things happen to us and we're helpless.

I believe Rotter's theory is relevant to the PIMO. When I meet a PIMO who's about to snap, their palpable tension is a result of waiting for outside factors to change before they can be happy. My question is, what if your family never wakes up? What do you do? What happens next? You're 80 years old and your family still hasn't woken up: what did you do with the time?

Don't misunderstand me—I know what it's like to want your family free of the stranglehold. I'm only suggesting that a small shift in perspective can help to bridge the gap between how you feel now and finding the happiness you deserve.

Body Tracking

Our bodies send us signals all the time: when we're hungry, tired, anxious, amorous. Watchtower taught you to fight your natural instincts and intuition, but your body is smart and will beat you every time. When you find yourself at a crossroads or facing a tough decision, what sensations do you experience? Does your blood pressure rise? Does your neck tense? What correlations do you notice between these sensations and your environment? What are the circumstances—the who, what, when, where—that incite this response? Finally, what are you going to do about it?

Risk

In NBC's *The Office*, socially inept branch manager Michael Scott subjects his employees to all sorts of shenanigans. In one episode, Scott impersonates Willy Wonka, complete with cane and top hat, as he implements an incentive program using golden tickets. In typical fashion, his plan goes awry and he lands himself in hot water with Chief Financial Officer David Wallace. Terrified that a confession will cost him his job, Scott tries to manipulate the office kiss-ass into taking the heat.

In a sudden plot twist, however, Scott's golden ticket snafu ends up paying greater dividends than expected, leading Wallace to reward the mastermind behind the original initiative. After throwing his employee under the bus only moments before the great news, Scott tries to claim that he's responsible for the brilliant idea, igniting a stubborn debate between the two. When Wallace asks Scott how he proposes to resolve the issue, Scott replies, "Well, David, I will be honest with you. I do want the credit without any of the blame."

When a PIMO comes to me in desperation and asks, *What should I do?*, meaning, they don't know whether they should leave the organization or stay, I don't believe them. I believe they know exactly what to do, but are resisting accountability. Here's the deal: if I tell you to leave the organization and your life falls apart, it's too easy to point the finger and divest yourself of any responsibility. Conversely, if I tell you to stay in the organization and you miss out on life-changing opportunities, your reaction is the same—it's someone else's fault that you have regrets.

Watchtower forced you to hold their hand and in the process of trying to pry yourself loose, you're looking to someone else to do the job. I'm not going to hold your hand, and it's not because I'm being dismissive, or because I get something out of watching you struggle. Rather, I'm giving you the credit Watchtower never will: that you're a reasonable person capable of making good decisions most of the time. As with any risk, you're going to find what works for you and what doesn't, and you'll grow more comfortable with the fact that no one has all the answers. But to relieve you of that risk is to potentially rob you of the victory that's rightfully yours.

THE THERAPY PART

"You're Going to Explode"

During the initial phase of my exit, I didn't know just how much pent-up anger I had until I went to a local homeopathic doctor. I was seeking treatment for depression, but didn't acknowledge it as such. Instead, I stumbled through a description of symptoms, choosing my words carefully so as not to give away my identity as a Jehovah's Witness. Even though I felt unhappy and unfulfilled, I was always protecting the organization in my conversations with "worldly" people. I didn't speak negatively about the organization out of fear of "bringing reproach on Jehovah's name," essentially defending the thing that was making me sick.

In a failed game of Guess-My-Religion, she tried to deduce that I was Mormon, then eventually let it go. At the end of the hour, she prescribed me a vial of white pellets labelled STAPHYSAGRIA, and flashing her eyes wide, said, "You're going to explode." Based on the otherwise reassuring office visit, I didn't give much thought to her comment until two days later when I was throwing sharp objects at the wall and hyperventilating.

Apparently, *staphysagria* was prescribed for repressed emotions, and as a Jehovah's Witness, I had plenty.

Emotional Rollercoaster

Your emotions are highly regulated when you're a Jehovah's Witness; you're not allowed to feel angry or bitter. You may experience grief, but don't let it linger. Taking pride in one's personal achievements is dangerous, and sexual feelings are dirty and sinful outside the parameters of heterosexual marriage. The only acceptable emotion is happiness, specifically, boundless happiness to be a Jehovah's Witness. Consequently, you learn to ignore your intuition and other warning signs that something is "off."

A well-trained Jehovah's Witness would point to this and say, *See? You said it yourself! Those who leave are angry and bitter!* Watchtower treats these emotions like character defects rather than natural reactions to injustice. If you brought your car to the mechanic and they ripped you off, you would feel angry. If you lost your retirement in a Ponzi scheme, you would feel bitter. The degree to which you allow yourself to be enslaved by these emotions is one thing; but when you entrust someone with something valuable—in this case, your life—and they lie to you, anger and bitterness are appropriate responses.

When I started waking up to the truth about "the truth," I thought I was going crazy, but it turns out I just had a toxic reservoir of unexpressed emotion that I needed to unload. When you leave the organization, you may feel like you're on an emotional rollercoaster, and that's OK. Your ride might look different from someone else's, but without the usual constraints placed on you by your family and the congregation, you may find yourself expressing the full range of human emotion for the first time.

Mixed Reviews

My experience as an activist gave me insight into how former Jehovah's Witnesses view therapy, which included the following:

1. They were never educated of its value.
2. Seeking therapy means you're too weak or stupid to handle your own problems.
3. It's all bullshit and a waste of money (of course, *they* have the prescription for life).

These viewpoints aren't unique to former Jehovah's Witnesses, but there's no question the organization exacerbates existing stigmas. In an astounding demonstration of logical fallacy, one Watchtower article states, "Remember, there are basically two sources of information—Jehovah, and the world under Satan's control."[1] Suggesting that reading the Bible along with a steady diet of Watchtower propaganda is enough to cure what ails you, any who dare seek the help of a mental health professional are subsequently shamed. Therefore, one of my primary goals as an activist was to destigmatize therapy for former Jehovah's Witnesses, so they could get the help they need.

As for the third opinion, it has been my experience that those who are most vocal about the futility of therapy are stuck in Watchtower mentality. No doubt, I believe it's possible to have a less-than-stellar experience with therapy, and when you're paying your hard-earned dollar for something that you don't feel is effective, you're less inclined to continue. However, there is zero evidence to support that therapy has no value, and to shame others for seeking potentially life-saving treatment only perpetuates the ignorance you claim to hate.

My Case for Therapy

Therapy helped me in three key ways: (1) it allowed me to express myself without judgment, (2) I learned healthy ways of coping with stress, and (3) the more I went, the less foreign "the world" felt.

This last benefit was instrumental in helping me combat

Watchtower's Us vs. Them mentality. As a Jehovah's Witness, you're taught that you are "no part of the world," that you should "remain separate from the world." For many born into the organization, this kind of isolationism creates a sense of insecurity that's hard to shake even well into adulthood; for all intents and purposes, you're a capable adult, but privately struggling to find your place in the world. I realize this dilemma isn't unique to Jehovah's Witnesses, but I feel it's especially difficult for a group of people who have been conditioned to believe they're not welcome in the world of which they are, in fact, a part.

When you talk about your experience as a Jehovah's Witness in that first therapy session, it feels like you're stepping behind enemy lines, because you literally had the fear of God instilled in you to never speak about the organization in less than glowing terms. However, my therapist never tried to stop me from being a Jehovah's Witness. Their ability to remain objective and still show compassion spoke volumes; even if their professional code of ethics was the reason, this proved to me that it was possible for humans to coexist, and that "the world" was nothing but a construct created by Watchtower to control its members and prevent critical thinking. In this way, therapy was the first step in emolliating those invisible barriers Watchtower put in place to isolate me from the rest of humankind.

A Few Challenges

I'm not suggesting that therapy is the only way to connect with other human beings, or that it's required to reach these conclusions. Many former Jehovah's Witnesses have gone on to forge friendships and lead fulfilling lives sans therapy. I will further qualify my statements with the point that I view therapy as a good component of any wellbeing program, such as eating a balanced diet and getting exercise. Nonetheless, I've observed two challenges facing former Jehovah's Witnesses as a demographic where I believe therapy presents possible solutions.

First, former Jehovah's Witnesses all over the world have found camaraderie through shared experience, which I believe is a vital part of the healing process; not even the most compassionate therapist can fully relate to your upbringing like someone who has been there. I was so inspired by this community that I dedicated a year of my life to online activism. I'm proud to have participated in and contributed to a community that has made significant strides in exposing abuses of power, and I will continue to support those who sacrifice the comfort of their anonymity to speak up.

However, there's also truth in the adage, "misery loves company," and I believe rehashing everything in perpetuity to the neglect of personal growth can lead to a new kind of toxic relationship. While giving you the space to acknowledge your pain, the constructive nature of therapy ultimately motivates you to work through it. This isn't to say that you're some finished product, or "fixed", after an arbitrary number of sessions, only that therapy puts you in a better position to manage your trauma, rather than have it manage you.

Another challenge facing this community is the apparent lack of knowledge about Jehovah's Witnesses among mental health professionals. The former Jehovah's Witnesses and PIMOs I've spoken with who have pursued therapy express that their therapist "doesn't get it"; they find themselves having to educate the professional while applying salve to their own wounds. Though I'm sure these professionals have a general understanding of fundamentalist ideologies, especially in the United States, it seems that specialization in cult mind control is a different animal.

I've been reticent to use the term "cult" only because I know it's a triggering word for Jehovah's Witnesses, enough to scare off a curious reader who doesn't believe they're in a cult. I remember how fragile I was during the initial phase of my waking up process; even though I was happy to distance myself from the organization, I was still defensive when someone referred to it as a cult. After doing research, however, I had to face the fact that the organization did indeed fit the identifying criteria.[2]

Herein lies the catch-22: A former Jehovah's Witness may be reluctant to continue therapy because they don't feel understood, but it is precisely their attendance that I believe will increase awareness and cement the organization as a cult in the professional dialogue. By no means am I presuming to know all the personal variables that influence an individual's mental health. The presenting issue for a former Jehovah's Witness may have a chemical or genetic basis, or possibly have its roots in some childhood trauma. All I'm saying is, if enough people report the same symptoms after drinking from the same well, it might motivate professionals to see what's in the water.

A Psychologist Weighs In

During my undergraduate studies, I found abundant research on the relationship between Jehovah's Witnesses and the healthcare system, specifically regarding their policy of refusing blood transfusions. I also came across historical analyses of their persecution in Nazi Germany. However, I barely managed to scrape up two sources of peer-reviewed research, written forty years apart, that discussed Jehovah's Witnesses in the context of mental health.

In 1975, John Spencer published the article, "The Mental Health of Jehovah's Witnesses" in *British Journal of Psychiatry*.

In his study of Jehovah's Witnesses admitted to the Mental Health Service Facilities of Western Australia, Spencer concluded that Jehovah's Witnesses in this region were "more likely to be admitted to a psychiatric hospital than the general population," and were three times more likely to be diagnosed with schizophrenia than the rest of the population at risk.[3]

In 2015, Dr. Meredith L. Friedson found similar psychological distress in her Jehovah's Witness patients. In "Psychotherapy and the Fundamentalist Client: The Aims and Challenges of Treating Jehovah's Witnesses," Friedson notes:

> *"the use of fear tactics and promotion of hate are prevalent… what makes this even more emotionally hazardous to the recipient of these ideas is that they are presented alongside love—and the barely concealed threat of the loss of that love for the most minor of offenses. This threat is applied to thoughts and feelings, so that questioning the doctrines or acknowledging feelings contrary to them becomes synonymous with the loss of morality, love, family, god's approval, and eternal life."[4]*

I presented a detailed review of Friedson's article on my YouTube channel, *Stop the Shunning*. Her accurate and comprehensive analysis was met with overwhelming gratitude from former Jehovah's Witnesses who felt as though she had thrown them a life raft. Her closing words encapsulate my own hopes for the community:

> *"There is clearly a need for culturally sensitive psychotherapeutic interventions for former and current Jehovah's Witnesses and other Fundamentalist populations who are experiencing psychological distress. Such individuals who might seek treatment face many obstacles, including proscriptions against interactions with "outsiders," deeply held beliefs about the nature of suffering as a direct reflection of one's faith, isolationism, pressures for secrecy and silencing from the institution in order to preserve the reputation of the religion, and more. Future research needs to continue in this area in order to develop a deeper understanding of the ways in which overcoming these obstacles to therapeutic treatment can be approached and implemented."*[5]

Can I get an amen?

Short Circuit

I don't have the credentials to make any assessment or statements about your mental health, nor do I have any empirical evidence that being a Jehovah's Witness directly causes mental illness.

Based on my experience as an activist, however, I can confidently say that there is enough anecdotal evidence that Watchtower has tampered with the minds of its members and has woven a web of intergenerational trauma through its shunning policy. I advocate for therapy, not from the self-righteous pedestal of someone who is "well" addressing the "unwell," but purely from a place of compassion. Your indoctrination is the work of an inept technician, PIMO—I'm only saying that therapy might help you repair the circuit board after Watchtower messed with the wires.

THE PART WHERE YOU'RE FREE

Blessing in Disguise

Despite its devastating effects, my issue has less to do with the actual shunning, and more to do with the institutional abuse behind it. I would rather someone shun me because they sincerely believe I'm a negative influence, than shun me because they're being told to; the former would make their decision a conscious and authentic one. Truth be told, when a mutually respectful relationship is not possible, having your family shun you could be a blessing in disguise.

I have to walk a careful line here, because the shunning policy has literally killed countless individuals. In the name of "remaining faithful," Jehovah's Witnesses have forsaken their disfellowshipped family to the point of driving them to suicide. These individuals lacked the emotional and physical support to navigate the abuse, and I hold Watchtower responsible for their deaths.

Shunning, however, could also be symptomatic of an underlying issue. What is the quality of your family relationships? Do family members frequently use the silent treatment to resolve disputes? Maybe this isn't your first rodeo, so to speak. After all, shunning is simply a prolonged form of the silent treatment. Is it possible that you're fighting for a relationship that you know is unhealthy? While I don't endorse shunning as an effective means of conflict resolution, what if being shunned sets you free?

As I touched on in previous chapters, your family has their "stuff," but having self-awareness is the difference between being a victim and a survivor. You have your stuff too, and while your family is responsible for their actions, they don't dictate your worth, or how you choose to respond moving forward. Having the fortitude to transform your impending shunning into a new beginning is just one way of making lemonade when your family hands you lemons.

Make Your Own Party

Our difference in beliefs aside, my mother was always a wellspring of mom-isms, one of which I still live by—*make your own party*. In terms of a social life, her advice was the antithesis of the Pity Party: when you're bored, bummed, or lonely, take the initiative and don't wait for others to make plans or pick up the phone. In a broader sense, she was adamant that I create the opportunities I wished existed, rather than waiting for them to fall in my lap. Giving credit where credit is due, this mantra instilled a proactive mindset that has served me to this day.

Once you're out of the organization, how will you make new connections and create meaningful relationships? As a Jehovah's Witness, the congregation was your built-in community; love 'em or hate 'em, soon you won't have the convenience of feeling either way about them. Rather, you'll need to determine what it is you value in a friendship and how you're going to foster new friendships now that the social landscape has changed.

We Didn't Start the Fire

I wrote my first book, *Alive and Well: A Healing Journal for the Shunned* to honor the shunned and accord them the dignity they deserve. *Stop the Shunning* highlighted the scope of the damage: some shunned individuals have never met their grandchildren because their devout children are withholding communication; others weren't invited to their parent's funeral; and all have been stonewalled by a friend they were close with for years. Watchtower refers to activists and others who speak about their experience as "mentally diseased" in attempts to quash this sort of dialogue.[1] Statements like, *why can't you just move on,* are typical of the Jehovah's Witness who deigns to speak to an apostate, as if they have any right to regulate, question, or even breathe in the direction of my hard-earned freedom.

The fact is, we didn't start the fire. Watchtower has violated bonds so fundamental and sacred, they're lucky more "mentally diseased" apostates aren't resorting to the deranged retaliation implied by such labels. While I'll never advocate the use of violence or using activism as a vindictive campaign, your family forfeits the right to have an opinion about your life the moment they choose to shun you. Therefore, if you feel called to engage in activism, either online or through some other form of peaceful protest, do it. Your family has the right to live by their conscience, but so do you, and your courage to speak up may very well save someone's life.

Aging in Reverse

I once made a video called, "Aging in Reverse: The Case of the Born-In Jehovah's Witness." It hit a nerve—I received a flood of emails from otherwise stable, sensible adults confessing to a level of arrested development which, until watching my video, they didn't know how to articulate. Essentially, there are Jehovah's

Witnesses who come into the organization after spending their formative years in "the world," and there are those who are born and raised in the organization who are expected to be adults before they have the chance to be kids. Consequently, these purebreds who leave the organization find themselves playing a game of Developmental Catch-Up that's incongruent with their chronological age.

Jehovah's Witnesses who came into the organization as self-actualized adults were given the time and space to explore their sexuality, go to college, and have social experiences that challenge their understanding of the world. Granted, not all experiences are positive. Unfortunately, these converts are manipulated into presenting their pre-Witness history as an irrelevant or wasted chapter of their life in light of their newfound convictions. As for the particularly pious convert with a "wild past", it's easy to find God *after* you've had your fun.

Life is different for the born-in Jehovah's Witness. Like a pinched garden hose, their natural development is suppressed to the degree that they either snap and lose all sense of impulse control, or they struggle with blockages that prevent them from functioning as healthy adults long after they've left the organization. Even the seemingly well-adjusted of the pack are left with hang-ups that can be fairly attributed to their upbringing.

While I sympathize with any Jehovah's Witness coming out of the Watchtower fog, I'm inclined to have more compassion for the born-in PIMO since I know of the confusing transition period that lies ahead. How do you make up for lost time? How do you recapture moments you never had? For some, attempting to imbue meaning where there previously was none, doesn't work. My husband, for instance, doesn't care to celebrate his birthday; he never celebrated his birthday when he was growing up as a Jehovah's Witness, and no amount of birthday cake at this stage of his life can make up for the lack of nostalgia. For others, these previously forbidden cultural milestones are the perfect entry into mainstream society and creating memories with the time they have left.

Still, others experience an identity crisis in the wake of their freedom—*if I'm not one of Jehovah's Witnesses, who am I?* The core issue isn't about adopting a new title, i.e. I'm an atheist/artist/academic now, but instead involves challenging what we think we know about ourselves. For instance, as a Jehovah's Witness, I was required to interact with the congregation, as well as strangers in the ministry. Does this mean I was a genuine extrovert, or a product of my environment? Was I a good example because I loved the rules, or because I was too afraid to break them? What other beliefs or assumptions might I still be holding onto, and are they an accurate reflection of who I truly am?

Aging in reverse is a disorienting and inconvenient experience. *I feel like I'm a teenager again,* is a common post-Watchtower sentiment for those trying to figure out who the hell they really are. You may go through phases, or feel like you're stuck in a developmental purgatory for a time. Wherever you are in your personal evolution, trust that whatever it is you're experiencing is serving a purpose and needs to happen for you to grow. No, you're not going through puberty again—you're just becoming who you were meant to be.

The Cliff

This is it. You've done your research and applied your critical thinking skills. You determined this isn't The Truth, and you know you must get out. But when you look down, your knees buckle and your heart is in your throat. The wind from the gaping expanse whips around your waist, threatening to send you over the edge. You back up in a panic, promising to yourself that if you can just calculate your steps perfectly, you'll make it to the ground safely.

Trying to figure out every consequence of your exit from Watchtower is like climbing down a cliff; you're going to see every jagged edge until staying where you are starts to look more appealing. Watchtower designed it that way—your family, community, life as you know it, has you quarantined at the top, safe from the unknown.

I feel you, PIMO. I was on that cliff for years. I would walk the perimeter, trying to convince myself that I loved the view because the alternative was too scary. The fact is, you're never going to be ready to leave Watchtower, because being a cult, it has engineered your exit to be as punitive and painful as possible. Instead, I want you to look down at every rough spot on the face of that cliff, and jump.

I'm obviously speaking metaphorically, but I want to reiterate that I'm not suggesting you take rash or harmful measures in a time of crisis. If you're having feelings of despair, or considering suicide, please reach out to emergency services. A compassionate professional can help you wade through the soup of your own thoughts and put things in perspective when you're feeling overwhelmed. Remember, you're needed on this earth, and what may seem insurmountable now is only a temporary barrier to the better days that lie ahead.

I feel the cliff analogy is appropriate for the PIMO, because there are too many who, even as I write these words, are psyching themselves out from leaving Watchtower. The choice to jump off the cliff or climb your way down is a question of control; there are PIMOs who imagine that by carefully maneuvering themselves around their family's feelings and reactions, they can manage to exit without a scratch. But this simply isn't true—no one exits Watchtower unscathed. No measure of civility or thoughtfulness on your part will cushion the blow of disappointing your family, and you'll only exhaust yourself in this unsustainable dance. At some point, you must cut yourself loose from others' expectations if you're going to survive.

When you finally jump, you will release yourself from this burden of control. Yes, you're probably going to strike a rock on your way down or get poked in the ass by a rogue branch. People *will* say and do things that hurt you, and there's no guarantee that you'll see your family again. It's a long and scary drop—but for the first time in your life, dammit, you're going to know what it feels like to fly.

Remember Who You Are

Before I left for school each day, my mother would kiss me on the cheek and say, "Remember who you are." These parting words were her way of saying, *Remember that you're one of Jehovah's Witnesses.* The day after I announced my disassociation, my mother said to me, "Remember who you are," in what I can only chalk up to a moment of sincere denial. No, I never forgot who I was.

I was free until I learned fear. I was intensely curious until I stopped asking questions. I embraced the world until I was taught to keep it at arm's length, and I was complete until the Watchtower Bible and Tract Society told me I wasn't enough.

Remember who you are, PIMO, and don't apologize for it. Soon, you won't be physically in, mentally out. You'll be out for good.

RESOURCES

Recommended Books

Bridges, William. *Transitions: Making Sense of Life's Changes.* Da Capo Press, 2004.

Forward, Susan, and Donna Frazier. *Emotional Blackmail: When the People in Your Life Use Fear, Obligation, and Guilt to Manipulate You.* HarperCollins Publishers, 1997.

Leger, Bethany. *Alive and Well: A Healing Journal for the Shunned.* Barnes & Noble Press, 2018.

McKay, Matthew and Patrick Fanning. *Prisoners of Belief: Exposing & Changing Beliefs that Control Your Life.* New Harbinger Publications, Inc., 1991.

Websites

Freedom of Mind Resource Center, freedomofmind.com

JWfacts.com

NOTES

Introduction

1. Watchtower Bible and Tract Society of Pennsylvania. "The Truth Brings, "Not Peace, but a Sword."" *The Watchtower Announcing Jehovah's Kingdom (Study Edition)*, October, 2017, pp.12-16. *Watchtower Online Library*, wol.jw.org/en/wol/d/r1/lp-e/2017603.

2. Watchtower Bible and Tract Society of Pennsylvania. "Keep Busy During "the Last Days."" *The Watchtower Announcing Jehovah's Kingdom (Study Edition)*, October, 2019, pp.8-13. *Watchtower Online Library*, wol.jw.org/en/wol/d/r1/lp-e/2019602.

3. Watchtower Bible and Tract Society of Pennsylvania. "Is It Wrong to Change Your Religion?" *Awake!*, July, 2009, pp.28-29. *Watchtower Online Library*, wol.jw.org/en/wol/d/r1/lp-e/102009251.

The Fun Part

1. Watchtower Bible and Tract Society of Pennsylvania. "How We Strip Off and Keep Off the Old Personality." *The Watchtower Announcing Jehovah's Kingdom (Simplified Edition)*, August, 2017, pp.15-20. *Watchtower Online Library*, wol.jw.org/en/wol/d/r1/lp-e/402017525.

2. Watchtower Bible and Tract Society of Pennsylvania. "What Kind of Love Brings True Happiness?" *The Watchtower Announcing Jehovah's Kingdom (Study Edition)*, January, 2018, pp.22-26. *Watchtower Online Library*, wol.jw.org/en/wol/d/r1/lp-e/2018246.

The Not-So-Fun-Part

1. Lancer, Darlene. "Covert Tactics Manipulators Use to Control and Confuse You." *Psychology Today*, 02 July 2019, www.psychologytoday.com/us/blog/toxic-relationships/201907/covert-tactics-manipulators-use-control-and-confuse-you.

2. Moceanu, Dominique. *Off Balance: A Memoir*. Touchstone, 2012.

3. Gerrig, Richard J. *Psychology and Life*. 20th ed., Pearson, 2013.

The Therapy Part

1. Watchtower Bible and Tract Society of Pennsylvania. "Who Molds Your Thinking?" *The Watchtower Announcing Jehovah's Kingdom (Study Edition)*, November, 2018, pp.18-22. *Watchtower Online Library*, wol.jw.org/en/wol/d/r1/lp-e/2018642.

2. To determine if I was in a cult, I used the BITE model developed by Steven Hassan. Freedom of Mind Resource Center. "Steven Hassan's BITE Model." *Freedom of Mind Resource Center*, freedomofmind.com/bite-model/.

3. Spencer, John. "The Mental Health of Jehovah's Witnesses." *British Journal of Psychiatry*, vol. 126, no. 6, 1975, pp. 556-559. Cambridge Core, https://www-cambridge-org.ezproxy1.lib.asu.edu/core/journals/the-british-journal-of-psychiatry/article/mental-health-of-jehovahs-witnesses/C3C3B14DA9C1DA3D9A699E2D1F5CAC34.

4. Friedson, Meredith L. "Psychotherapy and the Fundamentalist Client: The Aims and Challenges of Treating Jehovah's Witnesses." *Journal of Religion and Health*, vol. 54, no. 2, 2015, pp. 693-712. JSTOR, https://www-jstor org.ezproxy1.lib.asu.edu/stable/24485364?seq=1#metadata_info_tab_contents.

5. Ibid.

The Part Where You're Free

1. Watchtower Bible and Tract Society of Pennsylvania. "Will You Heed Jehovah's Clear Warnings?" *The Watchtower Announcing Jehovah's Kingdom (Study Edition)*, July, 2011, pp.15-19. *Watchtower Online Library*, wol.jw.org/en/wol/d/r1/lp-e/2011524.

www.ingramcontent.com/pod-product-compliance
Lightning Source LLC
Chambersburg PA
CBHW072109150726
47999CB00005B/1965